Gate
HOUSE

The days

GW01465374

QUEEN STREET
BURY

by
Eric
Newsham

Copyright © Eric Newsham 1978, 1991
Drawings by John Glynn
Published by Gatehouse Books
         St. Luke's,
         Sawley Road,
         Miles Platting,
         Manchester
         M10 8DB.

Printed by L.V. Lawlor Ltd

ISBN 0 906253 04 7

Thanks to the Urban Aid Programme
for continued financial support.

Gatehouse is a member of the Federation of Worker Writers & Community Publishers.

Our House

I was born on 11th November, 1947
in Queen Street, Bury.
Queen Street must, at one time,
have been two rows of houses.
But by the time I was born
there was only one row
and that was the side with even numbers.
Our house was a two-up-and-two-down.
There was no electricity.
We were all gas.
Gas lighting, gas stove.
But the nicest thing I can remember
is the big old fire-place,
where my mother would bake bread,
and my dad would put the poker in red-hot flames,
and when it was red-hot
he would put it in a pint of Guinness
for his cold.

1

In the kitchen there was a coal-hole
under the stairs.
At the centre of the room was the stove,
and at the side of it was a meat safe,
as we had no fridge.
There was a stone sink and one tap,
and the floor was stone as well.
You might be able to imagine the trouble
my mother had just making the tea.

2

imagine the trouble my mother had just making the tea

The surrounding area was a sort of slum.

Well, it was compared with this day and age.

At the side and back of us was a cotton mill,

called Renshaws.

At the front of us was a piece of spare ground

which was called the 'croft'.

There was a row of houses and shops

with their back doors facing our front door.

Mother and Son

I lived at number 10

and the houses started at number 2.

At number 2 lived my Auntie Nora.

She wasn't my real auntie

but when she wanted any errands running

I would say to mother,

'I'm just going to the shops

for my Auntie Nora'.

Next door to my Auntie Nora,

at number 4,

lived a funny lady and her son.

The lady wasn't funny 'ha, ha',

she was funny peculiar.

Her son was no better.

He was tall, thin and streaky,

and was about 39 years old,

which I suppose was quite ancient

to lads 8 or 9.

His mother was fat and witch-like looking,

with bone sticking out of her nose.

Like all kids who see anything

out of the ordinary about people,

especially women,

they called her 'witch',

and teased her as such.

4

at number 4,

lived a funny lady and her son.

5

Now half-way up the street
lived Mr. and Mrs. Kenweathy.
Their son was married to my sister
and they lived with us with their daughter.
She was like a sister to me
as she was only twelve months younger.
We always went everywhere together,
and I always looked after her,
and still do.

Two Little Ladies

Half-way down the street
lived two little ladies.
They were extremely small.
As a matter of fact they were dwarfs.
I know you shouldn't laugh,
but when you are young
it doesn't seem to matter.

*down the street
lived two little ladies.*

But laughing apart,

they used to fascinate me.

I was always fascinated by them

and the way they used to get in

and out of the front door.

They used a long piece of wire

tied to the sneck.

When they used to go shopping

that was the time we kids used to laugh,

because the shopping bag was bigger than them.

7

The Dreaded Road

Right at the top of the street was a road,
the dreaded road,
because we were never allowed to cross it
by ourselves.
I remember once crossing on my own,
without looking where I was going properly,
and I was knocked down by a bus.
I wasn't badly hurt
and my mother would kill me when she found out.

The reason for going across the road,
in the first place,
was to go to the sweet shop
which was owned by Mr. and Mrs. Cliffe.
They used to look after me
in the summer holidays.

Right at the top of the street was a road,

THE DREADED ROAD

Mr. Cliffe drove a wagon
and I would go with him.
I saw some interesting places,
and I was always saying
I was going to be a wagon driver
like Mr. Cliffe. (And I was!)

Mr Policeman

I remember one incident as clear as yesterday.
And if I ever see Mr. Cliffe
we always have a laugh about it.
It was the summer holidays.
We were going to Liverpool
with a load for the docks.
Mr. Cliffe said
'Would you like to see a submarine?'
I said 'Yes.'
So he took me to see it
and we had a smashing time.

10

He said 'Come on now it's late

and we'll be late back

if I don't get my toe down.'

So he did and I said

'What's that noise Mr. Cliffe?'

He said 'Hey-ho, it's the police.'

So we stopped

and the policeman gave him a caution.

Well, Mr. Cliffe was very pleased about that.

So I shouted through the window

'Bye-bye Mr. Policeman!'

And he came back and booked Mr. Cliffe.

'Bye-bye Mr. Policeman!'

Noses in the Air

Anyway, getting back to the street.

Next door to us used to live

Mr. and Mrs. Davis.

They were from Wales originally.

They always seemed to be walking

with their noses in the air.

In all the street

there were only two or three with electricity

and they were one of them.

Mr. Davis would work till late at night,

or so we were led to believe,

(he was probably on the bevy).

Mrs Davis would come home about 5.30

and you could guarantee at least twice a week

she would lock herself out.

She would knock on our door

and ask me to get through the window for her.

So I would.

Then she would make the tea for Mr. Davis

and asked me if I wanted to watch T.V.

And I said 'Yes,'

as we didn't have one of our own.

Concrete Jungle

We leave the street for a moment

and, if you can,

imagine the places we used to play.

It was like a jungle of concrete

and factories.

So, our enjoyment was on the mill rivers

and in the mill yards.

It wasn't to steal anything

or to damage anything.

We just wanted something to do.

If we didn't mess round the mills
we used to go to Rochdale Road Park
which was about a mile away,
and then on to a place we called the Shores
(or its more famous name, The Seven Arches,
which carries the train
from Bury to Rochdale).

Jungle of concrete and factories.

14

A Little Devil

On the way down to the Shores
I would go to a shop which sold herbs
and was nicknamed The Herb Shop,
and still is.
The man who lived there had a dog
and I would take it out with me
everywhere I went.
I really loved that dog,
and if it can be that dogs can love people,
I think that dog loved me.
He was a little devil.
He had a bad habit of chashing hens
and people didn't like it.
Sometimes I'd be sat at home
and he'd come scratching at the door
and barking for me,
and my dad would say
'Your mate's here for you,'

15

and we would go out. By the way,
the dog was yellow in colour
and was called Sandy.

I really loved that dog

He was a little Devil.

Help, Help!

I remember when I was ill
and was confined to my bed,
which was down-stairs in the front room,
for a week.
At first it was exciting
to be pampered and molly-coddled.
Until I got bored and fed-up
with being in bed for three or four days.
Well, one day my mother said
'I have to go out to the shop for the tea,
so behave yourself while I'm gone'.
Well, she hadn't been gone two minutes
and I was looking round for something to do.
Then I saw the cigarettes and matches
and thought 'I'll have a go at them,
like my mother does'.

17

So I got them and put one in my mouth
and struck a match.
I huffed and I puffed until it seemed
like the whole room was on fire.
My mother never blew a match out.
She always shook her wrist until it went out.
So that's what I did,
or thought I had,
and threw the match on the floor.
I wasn't long before
the whole room was full of smoke.
The flames gushed up the curtains.
The window was fully alight.
And I was screaming 'Help, Help'.
Someone must have heard me
and sent for the fire engine.
Anyway everything turned out all right.

18

(My mother was in the green-grocers
at the time
and she said to the man in the shop
'I wouldn't be surprised
if that's not my little bugger').

I huffed and I puffed

Sadness for Leaving

It wasn't long before we were notified
that the houses were coming down.
The street was humming with excitement
and sadness for leaving,
as everyone was like family to each other.
First one, then another,
left the street to go far and near.
One day we got a letter to let us know
we had a house at Blackford Bridge.
So we went to see it,
and fell in love with it,
and that was the start of another story.

PUBLICATIONS LIST

Gatehouse publishes books written or taped by people who have reading
and writing difficulties.

SPEAKING OUT

LISTEN TO ME   £1.95   ISBN 0 906253 30 6
talking survival
23 A5 pages

SEE CURRENT BOOKLIST

"DISTURBING", "MOVING".
The writer takes the story c   experience of being sexually
abused as a child and goes   an adult. Gatehouse Books
is publishing this as a vital part   make public the long term
pain and distress heaped on to   house. It is an account
from which we can all derive hope,   h.
(Nominated for the Arts Council 'Rayn.   ing Award'.)

NEW TITLE

A GUIDE TO THE MONSTERS OF THE MIND
Victor Grenko   £4.
Gatehouse presents its first full colour publication. In a   **e,**
'A Guide To The Monsters Of The Mind' handles a seriou
Emotions, fears and scary feelings we all have, appear a.

32 A4 pages. Contains 45 full-colour cartoon illustrations by the   J
laminated glossy cover. Contains suggestions for uses of book and   mental
health organisation.

FORTHCOMING TITLES

TELLING TALES
A collection of short stories, poems and plays, written by students in Basic Education.
Suitable for a wide range of readers, from the adult beginner to the more advanced.

THEN AND NOW
A Resource Pack for reminiscence work with the elderly.
Written and compiled by Patricia Duffin.
Based on work with the elderly in hospital and sheltered housing, it provides detailed
examples and suggestions of ways of encouraging and developing memories. Includes
a copy of the 'Day In Day Out' publication.

COLLECTED WRITINGS

OPENING TIME: G. Frost, C. Hoy   £25.00   ISBN 0 906253 13 6
A Writing Resource Pack written by students in Basic Education.
341 A4 pages, 14 sections.

JUST LATELY I REALISE   £2.95   ISBN 0 906253 17 9
Women and men who came from the West Indies in the 1950's and
1960's tell stories about their lives.
96 A5 pages.

WHO FEELS IT KNOWS IT   £1.95   ISBN 0 906253 07 1
Writing by students from the West Indies living in Manchester.
26 A5 pages.

TIP OF MY TONGUE   £1.95   ISBN 0 906253 09 8
Women writing about their lives at home and at work.
22 A5 pages.

WHERE DO WE GO FROM HERE   £2.95   ISBN 0 906253 20 9
11 people tell how they survived as acult non-readers in today's world.
80 A5 pages.

DAY IN DAY OUT   £2.95   ISBN 0 906253 19 5
Memories of North Manchester from women in Monsall Hospital.
Oral History.
39 A4 pages.

WHO AM I?   £1.95   ISBN 0 906253 13 16
Writing about women's lives, selected and planned by a women's writers group.
35 A5 pages.

POETRY

YES I LIKE IT   reprint 1991   ISBN 0 906253 16 0
41 poems by new writers. Honest & refeshing, this book is a must for
anyone interested in writing themselves.
84 pages.

BOOKS FOR BEGINNER READERS

JUST MY LUCK   Frances Holden   £1.60   ISBN 0 906253 11 X
A short, funny story. "I should have gone to a wedding..."
16 A5 pages. Large clear print & line-broken.

TOO LATE   Frances Holden   £1.60   ISBN 0 906253 12 8
A visit to the dentist with a difference!
14 A5 pages. Large clear print & line-broken.

KEEP YOUR HAIR ON   Frances Holden   £1.60   ISBN 0 906253 14 4
The evening started in an ordinary way for Frances and Kathleen. Then something
unexpected happened....
16 A5 pages. Large clear print & line-broken.

(SPECIAL OFFER PRICE OF £3.40 FOR PACK OF THREE FRANCES HOLDEN TITLES. ASK FOR '3 BEGINNER READERS'.)

A GOOD LIFE   Alan   £1.60   ISBN 0 906253 00 4
Alan talks about his job and how for once reading problems can be a
positive asset.
12 A5 pages. Large clear print & line-broken.

AUTOBIOGRAPHIES

BAGELS WITH BABUSHKA   Hilda Cohen   £2.95   ISBN 0 906253 31 4
Poet, pensioner and feminist, Hilda Cohen writes of Salford between the wars.
63 A5 pages.

MY WAY OF LIVING   Carol Millbanks   £2.95   ISBN 0 906253 23 3
Extracts from a life. Carol, daughter, friend, worker, organiser and also
physically handicapped from birth.
64 A5 pages.

NEVER IN A LOVING WAY   Josie Byrnes   £1.95   ISBN 0 906253 01 2
In her moving story of childhood, Josie tells of her feelings as a child
struggling to cope with hardship and a lack of love.
33 A5 pages. Told twice, large line-broken print & medium print.

A WOMAN ON HER OWN   Margaret Fulcher   £1.45   ISBN 0 906253 03 9
In five pieces, Margaret describes her life as a woman bringing up a
child on her own.
20 A5 pages. Large print, line-broken.

(Nominated for the Whittakers 'Read Easy' Award.)

THE DAYS I LIVED IN QUEEN STREET, BURY   £1.60   ISBN 0 906253 04
Eric Newsham
It was just one row of old houses, but it was always humming with excitement.
20 A5 pages. Large print, line-broken.

LOCAL PUBLICATIONS

THE BEAUMONT WRITERS GROUP   Various   £1.45   ISBN 0 906253
Described as a 'refreshingly spontaneous insight' (ALBSU)
into the lives of the writers, all of whom suffer from cerebral palsy.
48 A5 pages.

FROM PEN TO PAPER   Various   £1.45   ISBN 0 906253 28 4
Words of experience from an older writers group.
48 A5 pages.

DRAMA

CHIPPING IN AT PRESTWICH   Various   £1.45   ISBN 0 906253 29 2
'Three skilful and amusing short plays' (ALBSU)
36 A5 pages.

Gate
HOUSE

The Days I Lived In Queen Street, Bury

Eric Newsham